All About my Mom

By:

K.A. Devlin, Contributor

Dedicated to my mom,

Mom's name↑

A note for grown-up helpers:

This book is meant to be completed by a child and presented to Mom as a gift. Moms always love getting gifts or cards, but those actually made by her child are the ones most treasured. This book, once completed by her child, will be a lifelong keepsake of the sweet love between mother and child during those precious younger years. Plus, this book rhymes! It will be a great reading book to add to your home library! Read it together often and have fun while instilling a love for both reading and writing!

While completing this book, your child may need some help reading or writing some of the words, or even drawing. Have fun, and let the child lead, but be there to help. It's ok if the end result is not perfect.

To Mom, it will be perfect no matter what!

I love you, Mom!
This book is for you!
I did all the art work
and wrote the words too!

This book is from me
and it starts on this page.

My name is:

and this is my age:

This is my drawing of you, Mom.
This is how pretty you are!

And this is a drawing of ME,
giving you a great big gold star!

These are 3 reasons you get a gold star:

1.

2.

3.

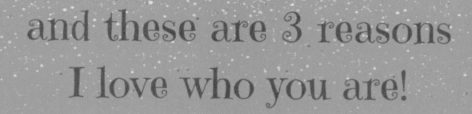

and these are 3 reasons
I love who you are!

Here is a picture of my favorite day,
the very best day that we've had!

These are 3 words that tell of that day,
what we did and why I am glad!

These are some flowers
I drew just for YOU,
all in your most favorite color!

These are some flowers
I drew for ME too.
They're like yours
but only they're smaller!

This is a list of 3 very best foods you make me sometimes when we eat,

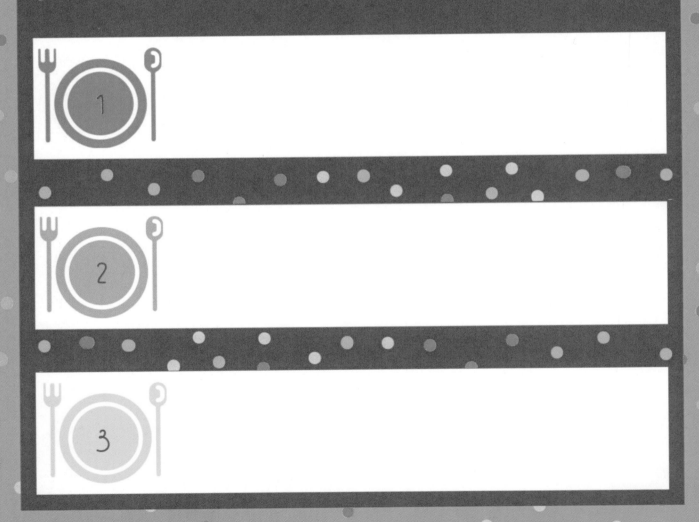

1.

2.

3.

and here I have drawn
my MOST favorite meal.
Your mealtime skills just can't be beat!

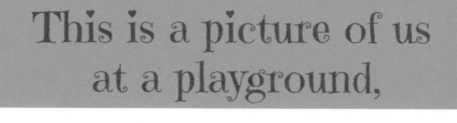

This is a picture of us
at a playground,

and this is a picture of us
when we're downtown.

This is a list of 3 books that we've read.

1.

2.

3.

I love it when you read me
this book in bed!

Roses are red. Violets are blue.

Here are **3** reasons that I'm proud of you!

If I could GET you anything,
this is what I'd GIVE you.

If I could TAKE you anywhere,
this is what we'd go do!

This is a list of some things about YOU,

Favorite
Song:

Favorite
Animal:

Favorite
Thing to Do:

and these are some things all about **ME** too!

Favorite Song:

Favorite Animal:

Favorite Thing to Do:

This is my hand. I traced all around it.

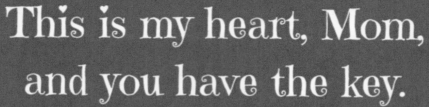

This is my heart, Mom,
and you have the key.

I'll love you forever!
You're the best mom for me!

The End

Made in the USA
Middletown, DE
04 May 2022

65256517R00018